REFRESH
YOUR
SPIRIT

REFRESH YOUR *SPIRIT*

A 30-Day Devotional of Prayer, Peace and Wisdom

ANGELA EUGENE

publish your gift

REFRESH YOUR SPIRIT

Copyright © 2025 Angela Eugene
All rights reserved.

Published by Publish Your Gift®
An imprint of Purposely Created Publishing Group, LLC

No part of this book may be reproduced, distributed or transmitted in any form by any means, graphic, electronic, or mechanical, including photocopy, recording, taping, or by any information storage or retrieval system, without permission in writing from the publisher, except in the case of reprints in the context of reviews, quotes, or references.

Scriptures marked AMP are taken from the Amplified Version®. Copyright © 2015 by The Lockman Foundation. All rights reserved.

Scriptures marked KJV are taken from the Holy Bible, King James Version. All rights reserved.

Scriptures marked NASB are taken from the New American Standard Bible®. Copyright © 1960, 1962, 1963, 1968, 1971, 1972, 1973, 1975, 1977, 1995 by The Lockman Foundation. Used by permission.

Scriptures marked NIV are taken from the New International Version®. Copyright © 1973, 1978, 1984, 2011 by Biblica, Inc.™. All rights reserved.

Scriptures marked NKJV are taken from the New King James Version®. Copyright © 1982 by Thomas Nelson. All rights reserved.

Printed in the United States of America

ISBN (print): 978-1-64484-660-5
ISBN (ebook): 978-1-64484-661-2

I want to dedicate this book to the Holy Spirit,
who inspired me to write it. I hope that as the pages turn,
Jesus is exalted and glorified.

To every woman who feels like she wants to throw in the
towel, I trust that the Holy Spirit will captivate you in a
way that will change your life.

TABLE OF CONTENTS

Introduction 1

Section One: Focus on Peace

Day 1:	Perfect Peace	5
Day 2:	Peace Begins Within	9
Day 3:	Peace Will Cause Thankfulness	13
Day 4:	Pursuit of Peace	17
Day 5:	Peace is a Gift	21
Day 6:	Peace Strengthens	25
Day 7:	Peace is God's Sovereignty	29

Section Two: Focus on Prayer and Trust in God

Day 8:	The Peace of Prayer	35
Day 9:	The Pursuit of Prayer	39
Day 10:	The Power of Prayerful Living	43
Day 11:	Effectual Fervent Prayers of the Righteous	47
Day 12:	Experience God's Presence in Prayer ...	51
Day 13:	Persistent Prayer	55
Day 14:	God Hears Your Prayers	59
Day 15:	Approaching God's Throne With Confidence	63
Day 16:	Withdrawing to Pray	67
Day 17:	Righteous Cry	71

Section Three: Focus on Wisdom

Day 18:	The Value of Godly Wisdom	77
Day 19:	Wisdom Preserves	81
Day 20:	Wisdom Requires Obedience	85
Day 21:	Living With Purpose	89
Day 22:	Open Your Mouth and Ask	93
Day 23:	The Fear of the Lord	97
Day 24:	Hidden Treasures	101
Day 25:	Strength in Weakness, Wisdom in God	105
Day 26:	Pursue Wisdom	109
Day 27:	From the Mouth of the Lord	113

Section Four: Focus on Obedience

Day 28:	Hear the Word and Obey	119
Day 29:	Do You Really Love Him?	123
Day 30:	Strength Through God's Word	127

About the Author 131

Introduction

The Holy Spirit impressed upon me to write a devotional journal, but I put it off. However, I am so grateful that although it was delayed, God still showed up in all of my preparation. I am humbled that He ordered my steps to complete it at a time when He was giving me sweet rest.

This devotional is intended for women who want to experience God's peace, find clarity through His wisdom, and enrich their spiritual lives through prayer. I decree and declare that after you diligently turn each page for each day and honestly answer the self-reflection questions, your life will never be the same.

In the mighty name of Jesus, amen.

SECTION ONE

Focus on Peace

DAY

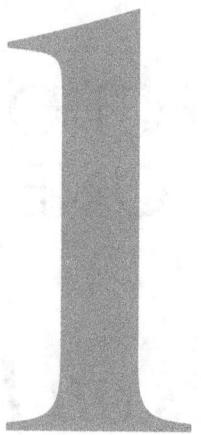

You will keep in in perfect peace those whose minds are steadfast, because they trust in You.

—Isaiah 26:3 (NIV)

Perfect Peace

Peace comes when we focus on and trust in God wholeheartedly. This passage, written by the prophet Isaiah, celebrates God's ultimate deliverance and salvation of His people. As a child, I used to dread crossing the street for fear of being hit by speeding cars. It was overwhelming, but I remember my mom's voice telling me to take a deep breath in and out while looking both ways. She always provided guidance and protection as she held my hand and reminded me that God was with me. This would calm my nerves and give me the confidence to face my fear of crossing the street. Similarly, this passage shows that when we focus on God and trust Him, His peace steadies us even amid chaos.

Perfect peace comes from the Hebrew phrase "shalom," which is a double of the word peace for emphasis. This signifies complete and unshakable peace, which only our God can provide. It is the peace rooted in trusting Him, not our external circumstances.

A steadfast mind reminds us that peace is given to those whose minds are stayed on God. This means a mind fixed on His character, promises, and sovereignty. It speaks to deliberate focus and reliance on God, resisting distractions and doubts. Trust is central to this peace. God's faithfulness and unchanging nature provide the foundation for lasting peace.

Prayer:

Lord, You promise perfect peace to those whose minds are steadfast, trusting in You. Today, I surrender my fears, distractions, and anxieties, choosing to fix my thoughts on Your faithfulness. Help me to rely on Your unchanging strength rather than on my own understanding. Let Your peace guard my heart and mind, calming every storm within me. Thank You for being my rock and Refuge, the one who sustains me. Teach me to trust You fully and to rest in the assurance of Your perfect peace. In Jesus's name, amen.

Self-Reflection:

1. What areas of my life feel chaotic, and how can I surrender them to God?

2. What thoughts or distractions are preventing me from fully trusting God and experiencing His peace?

3. How can I intentionally fix my mind on God's promises and character during moments of anxiety or uncertainty?

PERFECT PEACE

Write a Prayer to God in Your Own Words:

DAY

And the peace of God, which surpasses all understanding, will guard your hearts and minds through Christ Jesus.

—Philippians 4:7 (NKJV)

Peace Begins Within

God's peace starts within, surpassing our comprehension and protecting us from inner turmoil. This passage is part of a letter written by the Apostle Paul to the church in Philippi. Although Paul wrote it in prison, it remains one of his most joyful and encouraging epistles. The peace of God is not worldly peace but divine peace. According to the Merriam-Webster dictionary, divine means directly related to or proceeding from God. When you truly have the peace of God, it feels like a supernatural calm that goes beyond human comprehension.

I am an only child, and when it was time to step up and care for my father, I had the peace of God. It was not easy because our relationship was not outstanding, yet I had to trust God to help me in that season. Many of my family members were astounded by my ability to serve my father in the capacity I did. They were able to see the love of God through my actions. This was a gift from God because of my close relationship with Him. I needed to guard my heart and mind while serving and representing Christ. I had to guard both my thoughts (my heart) and my mind to prevent anxiety and fear from overwhelming me. Guard in this passage implies protection. This peace is only possible through a relationship with Jesus Christ. He is the source and sustainer of peace.

Please remember to replace anxiety with prayer and thanksgiving. Trust that God's peace will guard your heart and mind, no matter the situation. Always focus on Christ as the source of true peace.

Prayer:

Father, thank You for Your peace, which surpasses all understanding. When anxiety and worry try to overwhelm me, help me to turn to You in prayer with a thankful heart. Guard my heart and mind through Christ Jesus and fill me with the calm assurance that You are in control. May Your peace protect me and sustain me today and always.

Self-Reflection:

1. Am I fully trusting God with my worries and anxieties, or am I trying to control them alone?

2. In what areas of my life do I need God's peace to guard my heart and mind right now?

3. How does my relationship with Christ influence my ability to experience His peace, even when I don't fully understand my circumstances?

PEACE BEGINS WITHIN

Write a Prayer to God in Your Own Words:

DAY

Let the peace of Christ [the inner calm of one who walks daily with Him] be the controlling factor in your hearts [deciding and settling questions that arise]. To this *peace* indeed you were called as members in one body [of believers]. And be thankful [to God always].

—Colossians 3:15 (AMP)

Peace Will Cause Thankfulness

This passage illuminates how Christ's peace guides our hearts and fosters unity within the church. When peace rules within, it shapes our thoughts, emotions, and interactions with others. We are called to let this peace govern our decisions and emotions, allowing it to rule our hearts. In other words, it should guide our choices and settle our disputes.

This reminds me of years ago when I served on the telephone ministry in my former church. Our team handled calls from listeners who responded to our radio programming spot. We answered questions about the church's offerings and provided information on upcoming events and services. At the time, we had some conflicts within our team. The leader was not effectively communicating and did not have the best attitude. I had to decide: would I carry frustration and anger in my heart, or would I allow the peace of God to guide my decision? After prayer and wise counsel, I allowed peace to rule my heart by setting up a meeting with my leader to resolve the conflict.

According to this passage, the apostle Paul highlights that we are called to live in harmony as members of one body. This was God's design for the church as a place of love, support, and mutual edification. I am grateful I chose peace so we could resolve the conflict and reconcile our differences. Ephesians 4:3 (NIV) reminds us, "Make every effort to keep the unity of the Spirit through the bond of peace."

My heart was grateful that I stepped out of my comfort zone to confront a difficult situation. Thankfulness helped me to maintain a posture of gratitude to God. Gratitude shifted my focus from the struggle to God's goodness, fostering peace and joy. If you choose to let it, Christ's peace and thankfulness can shape your decisions, relationships, and worship.

Prayer:

Lord, I invite Your peace to rule in my heart today. Help me walk daily with You, allowing Your call to guide my decisions and relationships. Teach me to foster unity in Christ's body and always be thankful for Your presence and blessings. May Your peace be the controlling factor in all I do. In Jesus's name, amen.

Self-Reflection:

1. Am I allowing the peace of Christ to rule and guide my heart under challenging situations, or am I letting fear, anxiety, or personal desires take control?

2. How am I contributing to unity within the body of Christ? Am I fostering harmony or creating division through my actions, words, and attitude? (Consider your relationships within your family, church, or community and evaluate your role in promoting peace.)

3. Do I consistently practice gratitude, even in challenging seasons, to honor God and maintain inner peace?

PEACE WILL CAUSE THANKFULNESS

Write a Prayer to God in Your Own Words:

DAY

Turn away from evil and do good;
Seek peace and pursue it.

—Psalm 34:14 (AMP)

Pursuit of Peace

We actively cultivate peace, beginning in our hearts and extending outward. This passage helps us understand our conduct as believers in Christ. We should avoid sin and intentionally choose what is pleasing in God's sight. This involves not just refraining from wrongdoing but actively pursuing righteousness.

When I first became a newlywed, it was very difficult for me to learn how to submit to my husband in some areas. When I was single, I was very independent, and I was used to making decisions concerning purchases on my own because it was *my* money that I earned. Yep, very selfish attitude, right? It wasn't until I surrounded myself with wise women who poured into me and emphasized the importance of checking in with my husband that I truly understood its value.

One day, I wanted to make a purchase. I thought about just taking it and sneaking it into our home. I know you're saying, "Not you, woman of God!" But, yes, that was my thought. In that moment, I wanted to gratify my flesh and satisfy my want. Then, I heard the spirit very clearly say, "Call your husband and ensure this is an appropriate time to make this purchase." My former pastor used to say to married couples all the time, "Do you want your peace or do you want your point?"

I didn't want to hear the word no, but I chose to pursue peace and submit to my husband by asking his permission to make this big purchase. I could have chosen evil and the fleshly way out, but I didn't. To my surprise, my husband agreed with the timing of the purchase, and all I could do was thank God for giving me the strength to choose good and pursue peace.

I encourage you to live your lives marked by righteousness and peace, demonstrating your trust in God through your actions and relationships. It is a reminder that the pursuit of peace and goodness is an active, ongoing process in the life of faith.

Prayer:

Heavenly Father, thank You for guiding me with Your Word. Help me to turn away from anything that dishonors You and to walk in goodness and righteousness. Teach me to seek peace with others and pursue it wholeheartedly, reflecting Your love and grace. Strengthen me to live a life that pleases You, and let my actions bring glory to Your name. In Jesus's name I pray, amen.

Self-Reflection:

1. What area in my life requires a more intentional turning away from actions, thoughts, or habits that don't align with God's righteousness? How can I actively replace these with Godly behaviors?

2. Am I actively pursuing peace in my relationships or avoiding conflict by not addressing underlying issues?

3. How can I cultivate a deeper sensitivity to the Holy Spirit's guidance in helping me discern good from evil and equipping me to live a life that reflects God's peace and goodness?

Write a Prayer to God in Your Own Words:

_____

_____

_____

_____

_____

_____

_____

_____

DAY

Peace I leave with you, my peace I give unto you: not as the world giveth, give I unto you. Let not your heart be troubled, neither let it be afraid.

—John 14:27 (KJV)

Peace is a Gift

Trusting in Christ's unique peace keeps fear and trouble from taking root in our hearts. This verse is part of Jesus's farewell discourse to His disciples, recorded in John 14-17. These chapters detail Jesus's teachings, encouragement, and prayers for His followers as He prepares them for His impending crucifixion, resurrection, and ascension.

In 2022, my spiritual mother and I discussed an opportunity for me to work in full-time ministry. At the time, I was employed in government, and the Lord knew I was facing a lot of stress. We were short on team members, and the workload was becoming overwhelming. During this season, I was also caring for my father. I told my spiritual mother that I didn't feel God was prompting me to apply for this position. She suggested that we could pray and ask Him to guide me in my decision about applying. If He opened the door, we would know His will was being done. As the Lord would have it, another sister in Christ sent me a copy of the same opportunity. I said, "Okay, God. I see what You're doing here."

On July 31, I preached a sermon titled "Answer the Call." The very next day, my father passed away. Little did I know that sermon was meant for me when I reflected on this situation.

My heart was a little troubled because I knew navigating this new journey would be tricky. A few weeks later as I was making arrangements for my father's celebration of life, I heard the Spirit say, "Apply for the opportunity. It's time." I knew in my spirit it would be a significant shift financially. A few months later, I received the call to interview. The Lord's peace within sustained me after I obeyed what He asked me to do. In the natural and from the world's standards, this type of decision appeared to be a little crazy. Because of God's peace, I did not try to figure out any details; I left them in God's hands.

As I look back today, that was the best decision I could have made for my life. But I could not have done it if I didn't have peace that God would work it all out. It was also confirmation of a conversation I had with my husband a few years back about going into full-time ministry. The only difference is that I did not imagine it would happen like this. Isn't this how God works anyway? He does Ephesians 3:20—exceedingly and abundantly above all we ask or think.

Prayer:

Father, in the name of Jesus, thank You for the gift of Your perfect peace. As Jesus promised, let not my heart be troubled or afraid. Help me to trust in Your presence and rest in the calm assurance that Your peace is with me always. Please guide me in sharing this peace with others. In Jesus's name, amen.

Self-Reflection:

1. What areas of my life feel troubled or fearful, and how can I surrender them to God's peace?

2. How do I experience the peace that Jesus gives, and how is it different from the peace the world offers?

3. How can I live each day trusting in Jesus's promise of peace, even in difficult circumstances?

Write a Prayer to God in Your Own Words:

_____

_____

_____

_____

_____

_____

_____

_____

DAY

The Lord will give strength unto His people;
the Lord will bless His people with peace.

—Psalm 29:11 (KJV)

Peace Strengthens

God will strengthen and sustain us with His peace when we trust Him. This psalm connects the overwhelming power of God displayed in nature with His care and blessings for His people. Despite His unmatched strength, God chooses to empower and bring peace to His people, demonstrating His love and faithfulness.

My son was struggling at his job. He had a supervisor whose goal was to make him quit. She tried everything possible—from assigning challenging tasks to persuading other team members to join her in her disdain for him. She even sent emails with false accusations to leadership. The more my son took the humble approach and apologized, the worse things seemed to get in that hostile environment. As an HR professional, I advised him to document everything to protect himself. My son's advisor—who knew his character—couldn't believe how his supervisor was behaving. She encouraged him to seek other opportunities because nothing she did to help him professionally was effective.

Throughout this difficult season, my son remained faithful to the Lord, which wasn't easy. He chose to take the high road and maintain his humility. The Lord gave him the strength to endure despite the challenges. Each day, he had to work in a hostile environment. He applied for a position, and after submitting his application, the Lord blessed him with His peace.

God's power is a source of awe and a foundation for peace and strength in the lives of those who trust Him. It reassures believers that God is both mighty and caring, sustaining them through trials and granting them peace.

Prayer:

Father, thank You for Your strength and peace. In the midst of life's storms, remind me that You are in control and that Your power is always at work for my good. Strengthen me when I feel weak and bless me with the peace that only You can provide. Help me to trust in Your care and to share Your peace with others. In Jesus's name, amen.

Self-Reflection:

1. In what ways do I need God's strength in my life right now, and how can I invite Him to provide it?

2. How can I cultivate a more profound sense of peace by trusting God's promises?

3. How does recognizing God's power and care encourage me to face life's challenges confidently?

PEACE STRENGTHENS

Write a Prayer to God in Your Own Words:

DAY

Cast your burden on the LORD [release it] and He will sustain and uphold you; He will never allow the righteous to be shaken (slip, fall, fail).

—Psalm 55:22 (AMP)

Peace is God's Sovereignty

Like David, we will all face moments in life that drive us to lament in prayer. According to the Merriam-Webster dictionary, lament is a profound expression of sorrow, grief, or regret, often accompanied by a passionate cry for help or relief. This is also a form of worship—acknowledging God's presence and sovereignty during a storm or suffering.

As an only child, I often feared caring for my parents alone. Growing up without siblings meant I had never shared the weight of family responsibilities. My parents' loving but protective upbringing left me wondering if I was prepared for such a demanding role. Even after marriage, when my caring husband continued to shelter me, these doubts lingered. I was blessed that my very close aunt partnered with me when it was time to care for my father. Shortly after this season, my mom received a medical diagnosis that meant she would need my care.

Can I be honest? Here is where this passage hit differently. Putting it into action by casting my care of this matter onto Jesus was necessary. Based on the journey ahead, I knew I had to go into prayer and not allow this to shake me up. I cried out to God because I didn't feel I had what it would take to care for and watch my dear mom go through this journey. The Lord said, "Daughter, do you trust Me? You must leave this care with Me, and I will uphold you. I will sustain you and keep you." God did it. It was not always easy, but I was able to release my worries and challenges to Him, trusting that He would provide strength and stability in those difficult times.

This is a powerful affirmation of God's unfailing support for His people, no matter the difficulties they face. Peace is sustained as we trust God with our burdens, knowing He holds us steady.

Prayer:

Lord, I cast my burdens onto You, trusting that You will sustain me. Thank You for Your promise to uphold me and keep me steady. When I feel shaken, remind me of Your unfailing strength and love. Help me to release my worries and rest in Your care, knowing You will never let me slip or fall. Amen.

Self-Reflection:

1. What burdens am I holding on to that I need to release to God?

2. How have I experienced God's sustaining power in challenging times?

3. What steps can I take to trust God more deeply when I feel shaken or uncertain?

PEACE IS GOD'S SOVEREIGNTY

Write a Prayer to God in Your Own Words:

SECTION TWO

Focus on Prayer and Trust in God

DAY

Be anxious for nothing, but in everything by prayer and
supplication, with thanksgiving, let your requests be
made known to God; and the peace of God,
which surpasses all understanding, will guard
your hearts and minds through Christ Jesus.

—Philippians 4:6-7 (NKJV)

The Peace of Prayer

In this passage, we find Paul offering us encouragement and guidance on maintaining joy, peace, and contentment even in difficult circumstances. Paul wrote this letter to the church in Philippi from prison. Imagine never being anxious about anything. This seems impossible, right? We all have worries concerning some areas of our lives. Yet, we should worry about nothing and pray about everything.

Every time God would require me to speak in front of people, I would have anxiety about it. About a year ago, I was asked to be the eulogist for a family I did not know. I became a little anxious. The Lord reminded me that I must turn my worries into prayers. I began to thank the Lord for being chosen and used to serve this family in their difficult time of need. I asked the Lord to remove the anxiety and use me to provide comfort and strength as I spoke well of this family's loved one. After taking all of my concerns to God in prayer, I immediately experienced a divine peace that surpassed human understanding. Prayer and thanksgiving are keys to overcoming anxiety and living in the peace only Christ can provide.

Prayer:

Lord, I bring my worries and cares before You, trusting that You hear me. Help me to release my anxiety and replace it with gratitude for Your faithfulness. Guard my heart and mind with Your peace, which surpasses all understanding. I rest assured that You are in control. In Jesus's name, amen.

Self-Reflection:

1. What specific anxieties or worries do I need to take to God in prayer today?

2. How can I practice gratitude even in challenging circumstances?

3. In what ways have I experienced God's peace guarding my heart and mind when I've trusted Him?

THE PEACE OF PRAYER

Write a Prayer to God in Your Own Words:

DAY

Ask, and it will be given to you; seek, and you will find; knock, and it will be opened to you. For everyone who asks receives, and he who seeks finds, and to him who knocks it will be opened.

—Matthew 7:7-8 (NKJV)

The Pursuit of Prayer

This passage emphasizes persistence and your faith in prayer. Isn't it wonderful when God encourages us to actively pursue *His* will and blessings? If you're like me, there have been times when what we asked for was our will, not *His*, and we wondered why He didn't answer.

Let's break down the verse here and the part we play:

Ask – We should bring our needs to God in prayer with humility.

Seek – We should go beyond asking and diligently pursue God's wisdom, guidance, and answers.

Knock – Be persistent in your efforts, with faith, trusting that God will open the door at the right time.

Let's be clear: our God is not a genie, and we must follow His process, not our own will. For example, I applied for HR positions outside of my division. The interviews went very well, and I was very close to being offered one of the positions. According to His Word in verse 8, He said I would receive, and the door would be opened. It was my will to go outside of the division. However, God opened a door inside my division. He took me a different route by allowing me to serve in the department on what we called a rotation. From there, He opened the door for me to be transferred into the HR position I always desired. What am I saying? It won't always look like what we imagined.

God was faithful in responding to my prayer when I sought Him earnestly and in alignment with His will. He is ready to bless His children according to His will. Trust Him in prayer and action, knowing He rewards faith and perseverance.

Prayer:

Heavenly Father, thank You for inviting me to ask, seek, and knock. I come to You today with a heart full of faith, trusting in Your promises. Help me to ask boldly, seek diligently, and knock persistently, knowing that You are a loving God who hears and answers. Open the doors that align with Your will for my life and guide me in the paths of wisdom and peace. Thank You for Your faithfulness. In Jesus's name, amen.

Self-Reflection:

1. Am I consistently bringing my needs, desires, and struggles to God in prayer, trusting in His ability to provide?

2. In what ways am I actively seeking God's guidance and wisdom for my life beyond simply asking in prayer?

3. How can I cultivate greater persistence and faith when I feel discouraged or when answers don't come immediately?

THE PURSUIT OF PRAYER

Write a Prayer to God in Your Own Words:

_____

_____

_____

_____

_____

_____

_____

_____

_____

_____

_____

_____

_____

_____

DAY 10

Rejoice always, pray without ceasing, in everything give thanks; for this is the will of God in Christ Jesus for you.

—1 Thessalonians 5:16-18 (NKJV)

The Power of Prayerful Living

We have a perfect, powerful blueprint of practical guidance for Christian living, and when we do God's will, we will find it easier to be joyful and thankful. These commands are simple, but following them certainly isn't. We should maintain a spirit of joy, not based on circumstances, but on our relationship with Christ and the assurance of salvation.

Paul emphasizes the importance of a continual attitude of prayer. Having a lifestyle in constant communion with God. This doesn't mean being in prayer every second, but it does mean having a mindset of dependence on and connection with God throughout the day. Gratitude is the cornerstone of Christian living. We should thank God not only for our blessings but also in trials and storms, trusting in His sovereign plan and purpose.

I had to repent for the times I was unhappy about my storms and trials. The Lord reminded me to be thankful for His presence and the good He will accomplish despite my suffering. God's will is that we find something to rejoice for, something to pray for, and something to give thanks for. *Why?* Because it's *His* will. Adherence to these commands reflects a life centered on Him.

Prayer:

Heavenly Father, help me to rejoice always, pray continually, and give thanks in every situation. Teach me to trust Your will and to stay connected to You every moment of my life. Fill my heart with joy, my lips with prayer, and my soul with gratitude. In Jesus's name, amen.

Self-Reflection:

1. Do I choose joy, even in difficult situations, by focusing on God's faithfulness?

2. Am I making prayer a consistent and natural part of my daily life?

3. How often do I express gratitude to God when facing challenges?

THE POWER OF PRAYERFUL LIVING

Write a Prayer to God in Your Own Words:

DAY 11

Confess your trespasses to one another, and pray for one another, that you may be healed. The effective, fervent prayer of a righteous man avails much.

—James 5:16 (NKJV)

Effectual Fervent Prayers of the Righteous

This passage encourages us to confess our sins to one another; it promotes accountability, forgiveness, and unity in the faith community. Most importantly, confession brings about both spiritual and emotional healing.

We are reminded, through this Scripture, that prayer is a vital tool for physical and spiritual healing. It reinforces our reliance on God because He is our healer, and He wants us to support one another in our times of weakness. Effectual, fervent prayer highlights the passion, persistence, and righteousness required in prayer. "Righteous man" refers to someone in right standing with God through Jesus Christ.

There are many times in my life when I utilize my small circle to strengthen my relationship with Christ. I confess when I am wrong or when I have missed the mark. I ask for prayer so I can be healed and forgiven by Christ. I understand that prayer is not a ritual but a powerful means of connecting with the Father and inviting Him to show up and show out! Aligning our prayers with God's will can produce tremendous and meaningful results. For example, in early 2024, I prayed for my mother not to have a procedure the doctors said she might have to have. I felt the procedure would do more harm than good. I solicited my circle to stand in agreement with me, and because of the effectual prayers of the righteous, God granted my request.

Prayer:

Heavenly Father, I come before You with a humble heart. Please help me to confess my faults and seek reconciliation with others. Teach me to pray fervently and with faith, knowing that You hear the prayers of the righteous. Strengthen my spirit, heal my heart, and use my prayers to bring Your will to pass. In Jesus's name, amen.

Self-Reflection:

1. What is one area of my life where I can seek growth or healing through prayer and faith?

2. How can I be more open and honest in my relationship with God and others?

3. Am I consistently praying with faith, believing in God's power to bring about change?

EFFECTUAL FERVENT PRAYERS OF THE RIGHTEOUS

Write a Prayer to God in Your Own Words:

DAY 12

The Lord *is* near to all who call upon Him,
To all who call upon Him in truth.

—Psalm 145:18 (NKJV)

Experience God's Presence in Prayer

God is always accessible and attentive to those who seek Him sincerely and truthfully. Call on God, not just in your times of trouble and distress but with genuine faith, humility, and honesty, approaching Him sincerely rather than with hypocrisy or pretense.

Many times, we say we're too busy to spend time with our Father. But just like any relationship, you'll only know He's close if you take time to build that connection. We often call this our "quiet time" with the Lord. I remember when I was younger and liked someone, I would make sure to call them and spend time with them because I wanted to know everything about them. I was intentional about building that relationship. God wants the same from us. He wants us to seek Him daily, on purpose.

It is crucial to call on Him in truth. In other words, we must approach God with a sincere heart, acknowledging His holiness and authority. I have to admit, there have been times I did a quick drive-by prayer, and I wasn't as sincere. I needed God to do something quickly, but that was not the appropriate way to approach Him. Can you relate?

God's faithfulness and reliability are beyond what we can express or imagine. He fulfills His promises and is near to those who earnestly seek Him. He is always ready to hear and respond when we come to Him with true faith and a heart aligned with His will. The more you have "quiet time" with God, the more you develop an intimate, honest relationship with Him through your prayers and worship.

Prayer:

Heavenly Father, thank You for being near to all who call on You in truth. Help me to seek You with a sincere heart and trust in Your faithfulness. Draw me closer to Your presence as I call on Your name. In Jesus's name, amen.

Self-Reflection:

1. What does it mean to call on God "in truth" in my own life?

2. How have I experienced God's nearness during times of prayer?

3. What steps can I take to seek God with greater sincerity and trust?

EXPERIENCE GOD'S PRESENCE IN PRAYER

Write a Prayer to God in Your Own Words:

DAY 13

Then He spoke a parable to them, that men always ought to pray and not lose heart . . .

—Luke 18:1 (NKJV)

Persistent Prayer

When we read this passage, we can see it's straightforward and extremely powerful. Jesus asks that we remain steadfast and persistent in prayer, not losing heart or becoming discouraged when His answers are delayed. We can trust that God will respond with righteousness and compassion to our prayers. He hears our prayers immediately. However, His timing may differ from our expectations. Our faith requires trusting Him in seasons of waiting.

My son and I were in prayer about the sale of his condo. We pray every morning before both of us start our day. In the natural, this request seemed a little bleak. Some would say condos can be a challenging sale because of the kind of loan a buyer has, and in some cases, there is delinquency in the condo fees from current owners. These are just a few reasons why some would give weight to the challenge of the sale. We both decided we would be persistent in our prayers and remain unwavering in our faith. I also solicited prayer partners and friends to join me in this petition.

After persistently praying for a few months with many showings but no interest, my son called me one day and said, "Mom, can you pray? A buyer is looking at the condo unit below mine and he wants to look at my unit too." My son also asked his sister to join in on the prayer. I began to pray very specifically about this request. A few hours later, the agent contacted my husband (who is my son's realtor), and he submitted the offer. Prayer works, and we believe God.

We must maintain a lifestyle of consistent and persistent prayer, especially in times of discouragement and delay. My son was discouraged along the way, and I had to encourage him not to waver. God reassures us that He hears and responds to our cries and reminds us that faith, patience, and perseverance are essential to a more vigorous prayer life.

Prayer:

Heavenly Father, thank You for reminding us to pray always and not lose heart. Strengthen our faith and perseverance as we trust in Your perfect timing. Help us to remain steadfast in prayer, knowing that You are faithful and just. In Jesus's name, amen.

Self-Reflection:

1. How can I cultivate a habit of persistent prayer in my daily life?

2. What situations in my life require me to trust God's timing and not give up on prayer?

3. How does this passage help me to trust God more?

PERSISTENT PRAYER

Write a Prayer to God in Your Own Words:

DAY 14

Then you will call on Me and you will come and pray to Me, and I will hear [your voice] and I will listen to you.

—Jeremiah 29:12 (AMP)

God Hears Your Prayers

Have you ever had a situation where your first response was to immediately pick up the phone and call your mom, dad, friend, sister, or brother? We all have found ourselves in situations where this is our natural reaction. There have been many occasions when I was upset and going through a difficult time, but I could not get anyone on the phone. The only thing I could do was call upon the name of the Lord and pray to Him!

This verse is part of a more significant passage in which God, through Jeremiah, encourages the Israelites to remain hopeful despite their current circumstances. The Israelites had been taken into exile by the Babylonians as a result of their disobedience to God. Jerusalem had been conquered, and the people lived in a foreign land under difficult circumstances.

God tells us that we must call on Him, seeking Him intentionally through prayer. He highlights "pray to Me," which means He wants personal connection and communication. It is simple: He reassures us that He is an attentive God who actively listens to our prayers. God is always ready to respond to genuine, heartfelt prayer when we choose to seek Him earnestly.

Prayer:

Lord, thank You for always hearing me when I call and for listening to my prayers. Help me to seek You earnestly and trust in Your plans for my life. Teach me to rest in the assurance that You are near and attentive. In Jesus's name, amen.

Self-Reflection:

1. Am I intentional about praying to God, even during challenging times?

2. How can I deepen my trust that God hears and listens to my prayers?

3. In what ways can I seek God more earnestly in my daily life?

GOD HEARS YOUR PRAYERS

Write a Prayer to God in Your Own Words:

DAY 15

Let us therefore come boldly to the throne of grace, that we may obtain mercy and find grace to help in time of need.

—Hebrews 4:16 (NKJV)

Approaching God's Throne With Confidence

Oftentimes, some of us come to God's throne lacking confidence and boldness. Jesus is our High Priest, and this text emphasizes His role as both divine and empathetic to our human struggles. We are encouraged to confidently approach God because of Jesus's work on our behalf. Because of Jesus, we can confidently seek God's presence in prayer and worship.

The throne of grace reflects God's authority and His desire to provide mercy and grace to those who seek Him. We are encouraged to rely on God's mercy and grace in times of spiritual, emotional, or physical needs. Knowing that Jesus understands our struggles provides comfort and assurance that He will intercede on our behalf.

I must do an attitude check when I think of confidence and boldness in approaching God's throne. My attitude should be postured to reverence Him. I remember a time in my walk when I failed miserably and knew I needed to pray and ask God for His grace and mercy. This passage stuck out to me during that season because I was reminded that I can enter into His presence without fear. Besides, let's be clear: God is all-knowing and powerful. He saw my behavior and response, so there was no fooling Him anyway. I am so grateful it is because of His mercies we are not consumed. He is our *help* in our times of trouble and need. God is accessible and always ready to provide us with help through Christ.

Prayer:

Heavenly Father, I come boldly to Your throne of grace, trusting in Your mercy and seeking Your help. Thank You, Jesus, my High Priest, for understanding my weaknesses and allowing me to draw near to You. Please grant me the grace and strength I need at this moment. In Jesus's name, amen.

Self-Reflection:

1. Am I approaching God with confidence, trusting in His grace and mercy, or am I holding back because of fear or doubt?

2. In what areas of my life do I need to rely more on God's grace for strength and guidance?

3. How does knowing that Jesus understands my struggles encourage me to pray more boldly?

APPROACHING GOD'S THRONE WITH CONFIDENCE

Write a Prayer to God in Your Own Words:

DAY 16

But Jesus Himself would often slip away to the wilderness and pray [in seclusion].

—Luke 5:16 (AMP)

Withdrawing to Pray

Have you ever been so busy in ministry, work, and caring for your family that you didn't have time to slip away in solitude with the Father? Jesus is actively engaged in His ministry in this chapter. He performed miracles such as healing a man with leprosy (Luke 5:12-14), and He taught in large crowds who sought Him out for guidance and healing.

Jesus was popular and faced many demands, yet He prioritized time alone with the Father in prayer. Despite being fully God, Jesus demonstrated the importance of prayer in maintaining a close relationship with the Father and seeking guidance for His earthly ministry.

I am intentional about withdrawing from everything going on and separating myself from the busyness of ministry so I can pray to the Lord. As an ordained minister and associate pastor, there are days when my plate is extremely full. Serving the community and church members can be overwhelming; therefore, I have learned to steal away in prayer, just as Jesus did in this text.

If Jesus can set an example for us to regularly step away from life's pressures to spend time with God in prayer and reflection, then we can spend time with God too. Remember to make time for prayer and solitude amidst life's demands.

Prayer:

Heavenly Father, thank You for the example of Jesus, who sought You in quiet moments of prayer. Teach me to value time in Your presence, to find strength in stillness, and to seek Your guidance daily. Help me to withdraw from the busyness of life to be renewed by Your peace. In Jesus's name, amen.

Self-Reflection:

1. How can I create space in my day to spend quiet time with God?

2. What areas of my life feel busy or overwhelming, and how can I surrender them to God in prayer?

3. How does prayer help me to stay connected to God's will and purpose for my life?

WITHDRAWING TO PRAY

Write a Prayer to God in Your Own Words:

DAY

17

When the *righteous* cry [for help], the LORD hears and rescues them from all their distress *and* troubles.

—Psalm 34:17 (AMP)

Righteous Cry

There are times in our Christian walk when we face difficulties and challenges. Often, we retreat without taking a moment to cry out for help from the Lord. We must remember that the Lord is near. The Bible declares that He will never leave us nor forsake us. He wants us to trust Him even when we can't trace Him.

This passage reassures us that God is aware of our struggles and actively works to rescue us from them. Here, we will find Him emphasizing the relationship between the righteous and Himself, highlighting trust and reliance. Righteous in this text refers to those who trust in God. We are not claiming perfection; instead, we are describing individuals who seek God, strive to align with His will, and rely on His grace.

If you are a mother, you can genuinely relate to this: Think about every time your child cried for help as a baby or young child; you were there to comfort them. You were present to rescue them from whatever was happening. In other words, if they were hungry or needed a diaper change, you knew in your heart that was their need and struggle at that moment. Jesus is the same way; He hears our cries and will rescue us from all troubles and distress.

God's character is compassion, and He is ready to act on behalf of His people. He can provide peace, protection, and resolution. I encourage you to read the entirety of Psalm Chapter 34. It invites you to trust in God's goodness and deliverance while walking in reverence toward Him. It's a source of encouragement for those seeking His help in the midst of their storms.

Prayer:

Heavenly Father, thank You for hearing me when I cry out to You. I trust in Your love and faithfulness to rescue me from every trouble. Help me to find peace in Your presence and to walk in Your ways. Strengthen my faith and remind me that You are always near. In Jesus's name, amen.

Self-Reflection:

1. When was the last time I cried out to God in my distress? How did I experience His presence or deliverance?

2. In what areas of my life do I need to surrender to God fully, trusting Him to rescue and guide me?

3. How can I remain confident in God's faithfulness, even when His rescue doesn't come immediately?

RIGHTEOUS CRY

Write a Prayer to God in Your Own Words:

SECTION THREE

Focus on Wisdom

DAY 18

Blessed are those who find wisdom, those who gain understanding, for she is more profitable than silver and yields better returns than gold. She is more precious than rubies; nothing you desire can compare with her. Long life is in her right hand; in her left hand are riches and honor. Her ways are pleasant ways, and all her paths are peace. She is a tree of life to those who take hold of her; those who hold her fast will be blessed.

—Proverbs 3:13-18 (NIV)

The Value of Godly Wisdom

Solomon was known for his wisdom. This passage emphasizes the value of Godly wisdom and the blessings it brings to those who seek it. When was the last time you sought God for wisdom?

According to the Bible, wisdom means both understanding the best way to achieve a goal and applying knowledge in a right and Godly way. It is a skill that's acquired through applying knowledge correctly. Wisdom is a virtue that's available to anyone. When we think about wisdom, it isn't earthly wisdom, but wisdom rooted in the fear of the Lord. We see that wisdom is greater than material wealth. It surpasses worldly riches because it leads to eternal rewards and a deeper connection with God. Wisdom is personified as a woman, reflecting her worth and beauty. Nothing we desire—whether wealth, status, or power—can measure up to her value.

Choosing to seek wisdom will lead to harmony and wholeness, steering you away from strife and destruction. Wisdom will teach you inner and outer peace.

I intentionally pursue wisdom by reading Scriptures, praying, and obeying God. I realized my way, will, and tainted perspective always make a mess out of things. The Lord had to convict and shake me in failed situations. I recognized that true fulfillment is found not in material gain but in life aligned with the divine truth, which is the Word of God. I must seek the peace and life of embracing God's wisdom daily.

Prayer:

Lord, thank You for the gift of wisdom that leads to peace, life, and blessings. Help me to seek Your wisdom above all else and to hold fast to its truths in my daily life. May Your wisdom guide my steps and bring me joy that surpasses any worldly treasure. In Jesus's name, amen.

Self-Reflection:

1. What treasures or desires in my life might I be prioritizing over pursuing Godly wisdom?

2. How can I bring wisdom, peace, and life into my daily choices and relationships?

3. What practical steps can I take to seek and embrace God's wisdom in my life consistently?

THE VALUE OF GODLY WISDOM

Write a Prayer to God in Your Own Words:

DAY 19

For wisdom is a protection *even* as money is a protection,
But the [excellent] advantage of knowledge is that
wisdom shields *and* preserves the lives of its possessors.

—Ecclesiastes 7:12 (AMP)

Wisdom Preserves

As we read this text, we find Solomon contrasting wisdom with other earthly advantages, like wealth, and reflecting on the value of these advantages in life.

Everyone needs money to meet their daily needs. Money provides material security, helping us to navigate the uncertainties of life. Wealth can address immediate needs, but wisdom preserves life in more meaningful ways. Wisdom provides guidance, discernment, and the ability to make sound decisions, offering protection from our poor choices or harm.

While money may shield a person temporarily, wisdom offers an eternal advantage. It preserves life physically (through prudent decision-making) and enriches life spiritually and emotionally. Wisdom aligns a person with God's purposes, giving them a deeper understanding of life's complexities.

Solomon takes his time to highlight the role of knowledge in enhancing wisdom. Knowledge becomes valuable when applied with wisdom, as it equips someone to live rightly and avoid pitfalls.

There was a season when I was dealing with pain in my left hip. I had been enduring the pain because I felt God would heal it and I would therefore not need to have another hip replacement surgery. The pain limited my quality of life and prevented me from being fully active physically. I kept ignoring the pain and making excuses for not seeking God on the matter. Some days, the pain was excruciating. I remember taking pain medicine more often than I would have liked. I made an appointment with my orthopedic doctor, and during the visit he said, "I am here when you're ready." In other words, there was nothing more for him to do. There was a decision that needed to be made concerning my hip. Finally, I went to God and asked Him for wisdom concerning the matter.

I had knowledge of what to expect because I had had a hip replacement years ago. I also knew the exact amount I was responsible for after my insurance covered its portion of the surgery. Now, it was a matter of scheduling the surgery, figuring out the timing, and ensuring my family would be on board to assist me during my recovery and healing season. God provided me with wisdom on what this would all look like. I immediately scheduled another appointment with my orthopedic doctor to select a date for the surgery.

After leaving that appointment, the weight of concern lifted off me. The Holy Spirit led me step by step, giving me the wisdom to ensure every detail was carried out with excellence.

For two years, I had been enduring this pain, hesitant to take time off work because I needed my full paycheck. But when I finally chose to ask for wisdom, everything fell into place.

Rely on God's wisdom as a secure foundation that can protect and preserve your life beyond what material wealth can provide. Choosing to have the hip replacement was the best decision I could have made using the wisdom God provided.

WISDOM PRESERVES

Prayer:

Heavenly Father, we thank You for Your wisdom, which serves as our proper protection and guidance. Help us to seek and value Your wisdom above all earthly possessions. Grant us discernment to apply this wisdom in our daily lives so that we will make choices that honor You and preserve our well-being. In Jesus's name, we pray. Amen.

Self-Reflection:

1. In what ways have I relied on material wealth for security instead of seeking God's wisdom?

2. How can I prioritize gaining and applying wisdom in my daily decisions?

3. Can I recall a time when wisdom protected me from a poor choice or harmful situation?

Write a Prayer to God in Your Own Words:

_____

_____

_____

_____

DAY 20

Therefore everyone who hears these words of mine
and puts them into practice is like a wise man
who built his house on the rock.

—Matthew 7:24 (NIV)

Wisdom Requires Obedience

Jesus uses a metaphor of two builders to illustrate the importance of obedience. When we hear His words, it's not enough to listen to them; the Bible declares we must be doers of the Word. We must act upon His instructions. True faith requires both belief and application.

Jesus represents the rock and the teachings of the truth of God. Building our faith on this foundation signifies a life rooted in obedience to God, which provides us stability and resilience. A life grounded in Christ is secure, even amidst life's uncertainties. We don't want to build our foundation on the sand, which symbolizes the instability of relying on worldly values, human wisdom, or superficial faith. When the storms come, they represent the temptations and challenges of life. Those who build on the rock will withstand these storms, while those on the sand will collapse under pressure.

This parable of building on a solid foundation has convicted me personally. While I have been diligent in nourishing my spiritual temple, I must admit that I haven't been obedient when it comes to caring for my physical temple. The Holy Spirit has nudged me, and God's Word has warned me about my food choices, yet I built an unstable foundation of poor eating habits over the last several months, resulting in unnecessary weight gain. Now, in this new year, I have genuinely decided to respond with obedience by intentionally making wise choices—choosing home-cooked meals over fast food.

Just as my journey with healthy eating demonstrates, every choice we make either builds on rock or sand. Ultimately, our foundation reflects our preparation for eternal judgement, as only a life built on Christ leads to eternal stability and fellowship with God.

Prayer:

Heavenly Father, Thank You for the wisdom and truth of Your Word. Help me to not only hear Your teachings but to live them out daily. Give me strength and discernment to build my life on the firm foundation of Jesus Christ. May my actions reflect my faith and my heart remain steadfast in You, no matter what challenges come my way. In Jesus's name, I pray. Amen.

Self-Reflection:

1. In what areas of my life am I hearing God's Word but struggling to put it into practice?

2. What steps can I take to build a stronger spiritual foundation based on Jesus's teachings?

3. How do I respond to life's "storms," and what does that reveal about the foundation of my faith?

WISDOM REQUIRES OBEDIENCE

Write a Prayer to God in Your Own Words:

DAY 21

So then, be careful how you walk, not as unwise people but as wise, making the most of your time, because the days are evil.

—Ephesians 5:15-16 (NASB)

Living With Purpose

We live in a world filled with dangers and dishonesties. Living a perfect life is impossible, no matter how much we desire or strive for it. We can get tripped up or ensnared by people, places, or things. We must be cautious to live our lives rooted in wisdom, using our time wisely. It is God's will for us to live carefully and cautiously, always matching our lifestyle to the teachings of His Word. Not to do so would be foolish.

Paul's letter to the Ephesians encourages believers to live wisely and reflect God's character in their daily lives despite the surrounding culture of immorality and spiritual darkness.

Our daily walk should reflect intentionality and alignment with God's wisdom rather than the world's folly. We should be using our spiritual discernment to assist us in all situations. We must make the most of our time, serving God and fulfilling His purposes. This passage reminds us of the importance of valuing time as a gift.

There was a time when my former co-workers were planning to hang out after work. A part of me wanted to attend so I could do more relationship-building with my team, but I knew I had to prepare for a teaching assignment for ministry. At that moment, I made the wise decision to decline the offer. Hanging out with my co-workers was not mandatory, and I felt the Spirit tug on me to make the right choice. My wise decision resulted in the people I was serving in ministry being blessed by the lesson I had taken the time to prepare.

We must resist the world's temptations and pressures, staying rooted in God's wisdom and truth. We must live purposefully and faithfully in a broken world.

Prayer:

Heavenly Father, Thank You for the gift of wisdom and the time You've entrusted to me. Help me to walk carefully and intentionally, seeking Your guidance in every step. Teach me to recognize and make the most of every opportunity to serve You and others, even in challenging times. May Your light guide me in a dark world. In Jesus's name, amen.

Self-Reflection:

1. Am I using my time wisely to honor God and fulfill His purpose for my life?

2. Are there areas in my life where I need to seek God's wisdom instead of relying on my own understanding?

3. How can I shine God's light in the "evil days" and bring His truth to those around me?

LIVING WITH PURPOSE

Write a Prayer to God in Your Own Words:

_____

_____

_____

_____

_____

_____

_____

_____

_____

_____

_____

_____

_____

_____

DAY 22

If any of you lacks wisdom [to guide him through a decision or circumstance], he is to ask of [our benevolent] God, who gives to everyone generously and without rebuke or blame, and it will be given to him.

—James 1:5 (AMP)

Open Your Mouth and Ask

Wisdom is Christlike. Asking for wisdom is ultimately asking to be like Christ. The Bible declares Christ as the wisdom of God. When we seek His wisdom, we grow in our ability to face life's challenges with His character and perspective.

Life is full of situations where human understanding falls short, especially during trials. Wisdom in this passage refers to the divine insight and discernment needed to navigate life according to God's will, aligning decisions and actions with His purpose.

Our God is a benevolent Father who gives generously and graciously. He is willing and eager to provide wisdom, but we must *ask*! We do not serve a God who scolds or criticizes us for our lack of understanding. Instead, He meets us with love and generosity. Indeed, this passage sets the foundation for a recurring theme in the book of James: the importance of faith. When we face trials, seeking wisdom from God ensures our decisions reflect trust in Him rather than relying solely on our strength or knowledge.

I remember a difficult situation that arose when I was serving in our women's ministry. One participant in the ministry had a conflict with another. As a leader, I had to schedule a meeting with them to resolve the conflict. If I can be honest, I don't like to see people at odds with one another. I talked with the Lord, expressing my reluctance, but I knew I needed His guidance. After consulting His Word,

I remembered this Scripture and began to ask for wisdom, specifically about how to open the conversation when we met to discuss the issue. The Holy Spirit faithfully provided the words to say, and we all walked away with peace and understanding. What's more, choosing to handle this situation with God's wisdom led to an unexpected blessing—one of the participants and I developed an authentic relationship that continued long after the class ended.

As our source of wisdom and guidance, God equips us to face life's challenges confidently, secure in His unfailing care.

Prayer:

Heavenly Father, I come to You humbly, recognizing my need for Your wisdom. Please guide me through the decisions and challenges I face today. Thank You for Your generosity and grace. I trust in Your wisdom and ask for clarity to align my actions with Your will. In Jesus's name, amen.

Self-Reflection:

1. Which specific challenge in my life right now most requires God's wisdom and guidance?

2. Do I fully trust in God's generosity and willingness to guide me, or am I hesitant to ask for His help?

3. How can I make space in my daily routine to seek God's wisdom through prayer and reflection?

OPEN YOUR MOUTH AND ASK

Write a Prayer to God in Your Own Words:

DAY 23

And unto man He said, Behold, the fear of the LORD, that is wisdom; and to depart from evil is understanding.

—Job 28:28 (KJV)

The Fear of the Lord

True wisdom is a gift from God. The fear of the Lord embodies deep reverence and respect for Him. We must acknowledge His authority, holiness, and sovereignty, as this establishes the proper foundation of wisdom. As I stated in earlier chapters, wisdom is not merely intellectual knowledge, but the practical application of Godly principles grounded in a humble and surrendered relationship with Him.

As Christians on this journey, we must understand that wisdom involves recognizing what is wrong and actively turning away from it. This reflects a heart aligned with God's will, desiring righteousness over sin.

Imagine you are a successful corporate business leader like Rachel. Rachel manages a large company. She is aware that her success and responsibilities are gifts from God. She ensures that her actions and decisions demonstrate her reverence for God and commitment to living according to His principles.

Here are some ways Rachel demonstrates her fear of the Lord in her leadership:

- <u>Reverencing God before making important decisions.</u> She prays, reads the Word of God (the Bible), and seeks God's guidance. Rachel attributes her achievements not to her skills alone but to God's grace and providence, remaining humble rather than prideful.

- <u>Turning away from evil.</u> She's presented with a business deal involving cutting corners or engaging in unethical practices. This deal could be lucrative to her business, but Rachel refuses because it would compromise her integrity and displease God.

- <u>Influencing others with Godly wisdom.</u> She shares with her team and encourages them to act with honesty, fairness, and respect. Sometimes Rachel faces criticism or challenges, but she chooses to respond with patience and grace, trusting God to bring justice and vindication.

Fearing God means honoring Him above all else, and understanding involves living in a way that aligns with His will while rejecting evil. I pray this example is tangible and practical.

Prayer:

Heavenly Father, Thank You for teaching us that true wisdom comes from fearing You and true understanding is found in turning away from evil. Help me to live in reverence of You, seeking Your guidance in all I do. Strengthen me to shun what is wrong and pursue righteousness, even when it is challenging. May my life reflect Your wisdom and bring You glory. In Jesus's name, amen.

THE FEAR OF THE LORD

Self-Reflection:

1. In what areas do I rely on my understanding instead of seeking God's wisdom?

2. Are there any habits, thoughts, or actions I must turn away from to live in greater alignment with God's will?

3. How can I show reverence and trust in God in my daily decisions?

Write a Prayer to God in Your Own Words:

_____

_____

_____

_____

_____

_____

_____

DAY 24

That their hearts may be encouraged, having been knit together in love, and *that they would attain* to all the wealth that comes from the full assurance of understanding, *resulting* in a true knowledge of God's mystery, *that is,* Christ *Himself,* in whom are hidden all the treasures of wisdom and knowledge.

—Colossians 2:2-3 (NASB)

Hidden Treasures

We wear many hats and have many different roles: mother, daughter, aunt, sister, grandmother, niece, and leader. Oftentimes, we tend to get caught up in the busyness of life. If we can be honest, our prayer life and quiet time with the Lord gets neglected. This passage reminds us that we must set our hearts on things above. This requires us to strive to put Heaven's priorities into our daily practice. Setting our minds on things above means concentrating on the eternal rather than the temporary things of life.

From his prison cell, the Apostle Paul writes to encourage the believers in Colossae and Laodicea, emphasizing that love will unite their hearts. It is essential to come together in spiritual strength, as the body of Christ stands stronger together.

As we see, wealth in this passage refers to the spiritual riches we gain when we deeply understand God's truth, which provides assurance and peace.

Christ is identified as the ultimate mystery of God. This isn't a concealed mystery but rather something revealed in Christ. All treasures of wisdom and knowledge are found in Him, making Christ our complete source of divine truth and understanding.

My grandmother passed away many years ago. I loved her dearly and miss her so much. She was a praying woman who adored her jewelry. When she went home to glory, she left me beautiful pieces I cherish as treasures in my jewelry collection. I felt honored to receive these precious jewels, and I never realized she chose me to benefit from them. This reminds me of how we discover hidden treasures in Christ, as illustrated in this text. What am I saying? Whenever I wear a piece of my grandmother's jewelry, I am reminded of the wisdom and knowledge she has imparted to me, helping me become a better woman in Christ.

The richness of our faith and all we need are found in Christ when we intentionally set our minds on things above.

Prayer:

Heavenly Father, Thank You for the treasure of wisdom and knowledge found in Christ. Knit my heart with others in love and strengthen my faith with the full assurance of Your truth. Help me to seek You daily and trust in the riches of Your wisdom. Guide me in every decision and fill me with peace. May I always keep Christ at the center of my life and walk confidently in His grace. Amen.

Self-Reflection:

1. In what ways am I seeking Christ as my source of wisdom and knowledge?

2. How can I cultivate unity and love in my relationships with others in my faith community?

3. Do I feel assured in my understanding of God's truth, or are there areas where I need to seek more profound clarity through prayer and study?

HIDDEN TREASURES

Write a Prayer to God in Your Own Words:

_____

_____

_____

_____

_____

_____

_____

_____

_____

_____

_____

_____

_____

_____

DAY 25

For the foolishness of God is wiser than mankind, and the weakness of God is stronger than mankind.

—1 Corinthians 1:25 (NASB)

Strength in Weakness, Wisdom in God

Do you know that sometimes, the Christian community experiences division, pride, and misunderstandings about the gospel? Apostle Paul does a fantastic job for us by highlighting the wisdom of God in contrast to human wisdom and the power of God compared to human strength.

In the previous passages, Paul explains that the message of the cross is seen as foolishness by those who are perishing (nonbelievers), but to those being saved, it is the power of God. What took place on the cross was significant, and if you or I were presented with this assignment, we would not do it, especially knowing that people would mess up and sin over and over again. Paul challenges the worldly pursuit of wisdom and power, pointing out that God's ways often appear foolish or weak by human standards but are infinitely greater.

Foolishness emphasizes that what seems illogical to humans surpasses the most extraordinary human wisdom. Likewise, what may seem like "weakness" (Christ's crucifixion) was more powerful than anything humanity could ever achieve.

In June 2016, I was on a flight from New Orleans, returning from a work conference. After we had been in the air for about an hour, I noticed that the flight attendants looked nervous and weary. I sensed in my spirit that something was happening that they weren't sharing with us. Shortly after my observation, the flight attendants announced that we were about to make an emergency landing. I immediately began to pray.

We all know we are supposed to save ourselves by putting on our own oxygen masks. I didn't know the person sitting next to me, but I grabbed her hand and ensured she put her mask on correctly. One might think that was foolish and not wise because, at that moment, the turbulence was intense and we were descending quickly. I prayed, "God, I shall live and not die." I also prayed for everyone on that plane.

We began to help each other slide off the wing. Again, I made sure my seatmate could get off safely. Others were helping one another as well. Naturally, this seemed very foolish; one would typically want to save themselves. I share this to contrast it with Christ's crucifixion.

How can someone dying save the world? He took the punishment for our sins so we could be saved. That was the most decisive act of love. What may seem weak or foolish to some is actually God's robust plan to save us.

Prayer:

Father God, Thank You for Your perfect wisdom and love, even when I don't always understand it. Help me to trust in Your plans, knowing that Your ways are higher and better than mine. Teach me to see Your strength in what seems weak and Your wisdom in what seems foolish. May I always rely on You and follow Your guidance. Amen.

STRENGTH IN WEAKNESS, WISDOM IN GOD

Self-Reflection:

1. Have there been times when God's plan didn't make sense to me at first, but later, I saw how it worked out for my good?

2. What does Jesus's sacrifice on the cross teach me about God's love and wisdom?

3. How can I trust God more when things feel confusing or complicated?

Write a Prayer to God in Your Own Words:

_____

_____

_____

_____

_____

_____

_____

DAY 26

Wisdom *is* the principal thing; *Therefore,* get wisdom.
And in all your getting, get understanding.

—Proverbs 4:7 (NKJV)

Pursue Wisdom

Have you ever had a season where you wanted to pursue something, for example, a degree, a certification, a career in a unique field, or personal development goals? You can identify how this felt and the steps and measures you took to accomplish these things. God is letting us know the importance of wisdom and understanding as the foundation of a righteous life.

Wisdom is the principal thing, signifying its supreme value above material wealth or human achievements. It's not just intellectual knowledge, it includes moral and spiritual insight from God. The Bible tells us that when Solomon was young, David taught him that seeking God's wisdom was the most crucial choice he could make. Solomon learned the lesson well and chose wisdom above all else when God appeared to him to fulfill any request. We should make wisdom our first choice. We don't have to wait for God to reveal Himself to us. According to James 1:5, we can come boldly to His throne and ask for wisdom.

As we look at the text, we see the necessity of understanding, which involves applying wisdom practically in life. This reflects discernment in making Godly choices. Wisdom is consistently linked to fearing the Lord and walking in His ways. It's through wisdom and understanding that one can live a life that honors God and avoids the pitfalls of sin. Let's prioritize pursuing God's wisdom, which leads to spiritual growth, righteous living, and an eternal perspective.

Prayer:

Lord, grant me the wisdom to seek Your will above all else and the understanding to apply it in my life. Help me to treasure Your guidance and walk in Your truth daily. In Jesus's name, amen.

Self-Reflection:

1. In what areas of my life do I need to seek God's wisdom today?

2. How can I prioritize gaining understanding through prayer and studying Scripture?

3. Am I applying the wisdom I have received from God to make decisions that honor Him?

PURSUE WISDOM

Write a Prayer to God in Your Own Words:

DAY 27

For the LORD gives wisdom; From His mouth *come* knowledge and understanding . . .

—Proverbs 2:6 (NKJV)

From the Mouth of the Lord

Let's be clear: wisdom originated from God. It is not something we can attain solely through our human efforts or intellect; it is a divine gift God imparts to those seeking Him.

We can find wisdom, knowledge, and understanding conveyed through God's Word—His commands, teachings, and guidance. If you are like me, there are times when we let our excuses keep us from seeking wisdom, knowledge, and understanding from God. In today's era, we live in a microwave society, wanting things instantly. Consequently, we often try to act as if we are God without truly seeking His wisdom. In other words, we must actively seek wisdom by obeying God's commands, crying out for understanding, and searching for it as one searches for hidden treasure. This diligent pursuit reflects a heart posture of dependence on God. God's wisdom is hidden from the rebellious and foolish, it takes effort to find it and use it.

God will protect and guard those who walk in His wisdom, and wisdom itself becomes a shield, offering discernment and safeguarding your path. I recognize that understanding and guidance come from living according to God's Word. Am I perfect in the way I live for Christ? No. However, I strive to be as obedient to His commands as I possibly can.

Wisdom is the spiritual treasure that equips us to live in alignment with God's will and navigate life's challenges with discernment.

Prayer:

Heavenly Father, thank You for being the source of true wisdom. Teach me to seek Your guidance in all areas of my life and to trust in Your Word for understanding. Help me grow in knowledge and discernment to make decisions that honor You. In Jesus's name, amen.

Self-Reflection:

1. Am I actively seeking God's wisdom through prayer and studying His Word?

2. In what areas of my life do I need to rely more on God's guidance rather than my own understanding?

3. How can I apply the wisdom I receive from God to my daily decisions and interactions?

FROM THE MOUTH OF THE LORD

Write a Prayer to God in Your Own Words:

SECTION FOUR

Focus on Obedience

DAY

28

He replied, "Blessed rather are those who hear the word of God and obey it."

—Luke 11:28 (NIV)

Hear the Word and Obey

This is a really simple command from the Lord. Jesus is speaking to people who highly value family ties. He is responding to a woman who acknowledges Mary as His mother. He directs their attention and focus away from physical or family relationships to highlight the spiritual truth that blessedness comes from hearing and obeying the Word of God.

A blessing is found in obedience to God rather than external or relational status. The Bible declares that when Abraham was asked to sacrifice his son, he was obedient, and God honored his obedience by letting his son live.

When we hear God's Word, we should not merely listen without response; we are responsible for acting on what we hear. While Mary is uniquely honored as Jesus's mother, this text extends the opportunity for blessing to everyone who responds in obedience.

Society often equates blessing with wealth, status, or relationships. Jesus reminds us that the ultimate blessing is spiritual—a life aligned with God's will. In other words, it is encouraging to know that anyone, regardless of their status or background, can experience God's blessing through obedience to His Word.

Every time I hear the Word of God and choose to obey, not only am I blessed, but it spills over to my family, mentees, and co-laborers being blessed. I would implore you to follow God even if you are afraid or don't have all the details of what He is asking you to do.

Prayer:

Heavenly Father, thank You for the gift of Your Word, which guides and nourishes us. Help me to hear Your voice and obey Your commands with a willing heart. Strengthen me with wisdom to align my life with Your will so I may experience the true blessing of walking in obedience. In Jesus's name, amen.

Self-Reflection:

1. Do I make time each day to listen to God's Word through prayer, Scripture reading, or reflection?

2. In what areas of my life is God calling me to greater obedience right now?

3. This week, how can I actively live out what I've learned from God's Word?

HEAR THE WORD AND OBEY

Write a Prayer to God in Your Own Words:

DAY 29

If you love Me, keep My commandments.

—John 14:15 (NKJV)

Do You Really Love Him?

Do you love Jesus? What does this look like in your life? As we meditate on this passage, let us understand its context and honestly examine ourselves.

In the preceding chapters of John, Jesus bids farewell to His disciples. These chapters capture His teachings, promises, and encouragement as He prepares them for His imminent departure through His crucifixion and resurrection. Jesus speaks about the relationship between love and obedience to God. Our genuine passion for Him is demonstrated through obedience to His teachings. This is not a demand but an invitation to align our lives with His will as a response to love.

He assures us that we will not be left alone. The Holy Spirit will guide and empower us. Have you considered the intimate relationship between Jesus, the Father, and those who follow Him? This provides us with an excellent example.

When I think about this passage, I understand that obeying and keeping His commandments must be a lifestyle. Please remember that someone is always watching us and we may be the only Jesus they encounter. Love is an action word, so it requires work on our part. Our love for Jesus is not merely a feeling but an active commitment to His ways.

Prayer:

Lord Jesus, help me to show my love for You through my actions and choices. Guide me to follow Your commandments with a joyful heart and strengthen me through Your Spirit to walk in obedience daily. Amen.

Self-Reflection:

1. Do my daily actions reflect my love for Jesus and His teachings?

2. What steps can I take today to align my life more closely with God's commandments?

3. How can I rely on the Holy Spirit to strengthen me when obedience is difficult?

DO YOU REALLY LOVE HIM?

Write a Prayer to God in Your Own Words:

DAY 30

Keep this Book of the Law always on your lips;
meditate on it day and night, so that you may
be careful to do everything written in it.
Then you will be prosperous and successful.

—Joshua 1:8 (NIV)

Strength Through God's Word

Joshua transitioned into leadership after Moses, the servant of the Lord, passed away. This was a pivotal moment for the Israelites as they were about to enter Canaan, a land filled with both opportunities and challenges.

We are reminded of the role of God's Word. The Book of the Law refers to the first five books of the Bible, which contain God's commandments and instructions for living. Please don't misunderstand—the entire Bible includes God's Word for our lives and is beneficial for living according to His will.

Meditating on God's Word is not just for knowledge but for internalizing it and applying it in our daily walk. God commands Joshua to meditate day and night, implying a constant and deliberate focus on His teachings. He asks us to do the same. When we are obedient, we can reap the promise of prosperity and success. This isn't just material prosperity; it includes spiritual success and fulfillment through alignment with God's will.

We encourage our disciples and mentees to have quiet time with the Lord. In our quiet time, we meditate on God's Word and allow the Holy Spirit to help us internalize what we are meditating on. This helps me when I run into challenges, storms, or difficulties. I can go back into my spiritual bank and withdraw God's promises and commands about what I need to do to be obedient in current situations.

God's Word holds power to guide, strengthen, and bring success when we consistently meditate on and obey it. This practice connects faith, discipline, and God's promises, encouraging us to prioritize Scripture in our lives.

Prayer:

Lord, help me to hold Your Word close to my heart. Teach me to meditate on it daily and to walk in obedience to Your will. Guide me toward the success and peace that comes from following You. Amen.

Self-Reflection:

1. How can I make more time to meditate on God's Word each day?

2. What areas of my life must align more closely with God's instructions?

3. How does trusting in God's promises give me the courage to face challenges?

STRENGTH THROUGH GOD'S WORD

Write a Prayer to God in Your Own Words:

About the Author

Angela Eugene is a Christian life strategist, ordained minister, and certified coach who uniquely combines faith-based teaching, coaching, and mental health awareness to support women in achieving holistic well-being and transformative spiritual growth.

Angela is an accomplished author whose faith-based writings have inspired countless readers. She has written *HerStory: Surviving the Journey Called Life Through Rejection, Abandonment, and Fear* and co-authored *Open Your Gifts, Volume 2* with actress and comedian Kim Coles. Her works provide encouragement and practical wisdom, reinforcing her authority in spiritual and personal development. Her expertise in spiritual development and personal transformation makes her a trusted voice in the faith community.

Residing in Clinton, Maryland, with her husband, Tyrone, Angela cherishes her role as a mother to their two young adult children, Jasmin and Nijel Eugene. She enjoys traveling, bowling, and using her platform to uplift and empower others in their spiritual journeys.

Learn more at www.nhimeyerise.org

publish your gift

CREATING DISTINCTIVE BOOKS FOR LEADERS AT THE TOP OF THEIR FIELD

We're a collaborative group of creative masterminds with a mission to empower leaders to share their unique knowledge, insights, and experiences with the world.

Our expertise bridges the gap between their wisdom and ideal readers—delivering impactful self-help books that inspire lasting growth and change.

Want to know more?
Write to us at info@publishyourgift.com
or call (888) 949-6228

Discover great books, authors, and more at
www.PublishYourGift.com

Connect with us on social media

@publishyourgift

www.ingramcontent.com/pod-product-compliance
Lightning Source LLC
Chambersburg PA
CBHW072210070526
44585CB00015B/1268